Travel Journal
Peru

VPJournals

Copyright © 2015 VPJournals

All rights reserved.

ISBN-13: 978-1518845192
ISBN-10: 1518845193

Contact Details

Name: _____

Email address: _____

Tel: _____

Address: _____

_____

Important Medical Information

Blood type: _____

Medication: _____

CONTENTS

Hi, I hope you enjoy this journal. It is packed with cool stuff and recommendations for you trip to Peru, and has plenty of space to record details of your trip.

What's Inside	Page
Before you go to Peru	
Great places to visit in Peru	6-7
Cool places to visit in Peru with kids	8-9
Good places to eat	10-11
Research Peru	12-13
Postcard & Packing List	14-19
Peru facts	21-22
Helpful hints	23-26
Clothes and shoe sizing charts, to help you get the right sizes while there	
Peru Trip Diary	27-111
21 day trip diary to record details of your trip	
Reflect on you Trip	
Summary of your trip	113-121
People you met	123-125
Useful Resources	127-136
Size conversion charts	129-132
Common Translations	133-134
Notes	135-136

Have fun in Peru

Great Places to visit in Peru

Qorikancha	✓
Museo Leimebamba	
Chan Chan	
Casa-Hacienda San José	
La Catedral de Lima (Cathedral of Lima)	
Caral	
Chavín de Huántar	
Monasterio de Santa Catalina	
Sacsaywamán	
Pisac Ruins	
Reserva Nacional de Paracas	

Huacas del Sol y de la Luna	
Ollantaytambo Ruins	
Yavari	
Islas Ballestas	
Reserva Ecológica Chaparrí Wildlife	
Machu Picchu	
Inca Trail	
Sacred Land Adventure	
Miraflores	
Colca Canyon	
PeruRail - Vistadome	
Magic Water Circuit	
Nasca Lines	

Cool Places to visit in Peru with Kids

Machu Picchu	✓
Parque De La Reserva (Park)	
Museo Larco (Museum)	
Uros Floating Islands	
Huaca Pucllana	
Marcahuasi	
Pacaya Samiria National Reserve	
Amazon Rainforest	
Huacachina Lagoon	
Cusco (Cuzco)	
Plaza de Armas (Huacaypata)	
Manu National Park	

Caral	
Pachacamac	
Historic Centre of Lima	
Natura Vive Sacred Valley Via Ferrata & Zip Line	
Planetarium Cusco	
Temple of Ollantaytambo	
Parque Nacional Huascaran	
Gate of the Sun (Intipuncu)	
Reserva Natural Marasha	
ChocoMuseo	
Parque de las Leyendas (Zoo)	
Enigmatik	

Good Places to Eat in Peru

Indio Feliz	✓
Café Andino	
Mar Picante	
Capuccino	
La Sirena d'Juan	
Magredana	
Fiesta Chiclayo Gourmet	
El Albergue Restaurante	
Mi Chef Kristof	
Buongiorno	
La Patarashca	
Malabar	

Zingaro	
La Olla de Barro	
KentiKafé	
Astrid y Gaston	
Cebicheria La Mar	
Panchita	
La Rosa Nautica Restaurante	
Central Restaurante	
MAP Cafe	
El Mercado	
Le Soleil	
Maido	
Zig Zag Restaurant	

Best Websites to Research Further

Do some more research on the internet to plan your trip:

www.theonlyperuguide.com
www.visitperu.com
www.perutouristinformation.com
www.peru.travel
www.go2peru.com
www.perutourism.com
www.wikipedia.org/wiki/Peru
www.twowanderingsoles.com/peru/
www.nomadicmatt.com/travel-guides/Peru-travel-tips/

More places I want to visit on our trip

1. _____
2. _____
3. _____
4. _____
5. _____
6. _____
7. _____
8. _____
9. _____
10. _____
11. _____
12. _____
13. _____
14. _____
15. _____

Postcard List

Name:
Address:

Name:
Address:

Name:
Address:

Name:

Address:

Name:

Address:

Name:

Address:

Name:

Address:

Name:

Address:

Name:

Address:

Name:

Address:

Name:

Address:

Name:

Address:

Name:

Address:

Name:

Address:

MAIL

Packing List

✓	This Journal
	Tickets
	Passport
	Money
	Chargers
	Batteries
	Book to read
	Camera
	Tablet
	Sun glasses
	Sun cream

	Toiletries
	Water
	Watch
	Snacks
	Umbrella
	Towel
	Guide book
	Kindle
	Jacket
	Medication
	Add more below

Peru Facts

- Peru is the third largest country in South America, after Brazil and Argentina

- Peru's capital Lima was once the most powerful city in South America, but fell into decline when the Spanish created a viceroyalty in Rio de la Plata

- Independence Day of Republica del Peru (Republic of Peru) is celebrated on July 28, and is known as 'Fiestas Patrias'

- There are 3 official languages in Peru: Spanish, Quechua and Aymara

- The local currency in Peru is the Nuevo Sol

- Cotahuasi Canyon in the Arequipa region is considered one of the world's deepest canyons at 3,535 meters (11,597 feet) deep, twice as deep as the Grand Canyon

- The Andes, the second highest mountain range in the world runs through Peru. The highest peak, Mount Huascarán, is 22,205 feet high

- Peru is the 6th largest producer of gold and 9th largest producer of coffee in the world

- The world's largest rain forest, the Amazon, covers nearly half of Peru. Nevado Mismi in the Andes is the source of the Amazon river

- Peru is a surfer's paradise. Chicama has the world's longest left handed wave at 4km's long, and Mancora (close by) has the world's largest left handed point break

- Lago Titicaca (Lake Titicaca) in Southern Peru is the world's highest navigable lake, and South America's largest lake

- Peru is home to the highest sand dune in the world. Cerro Blanco located in the Sechura Desert near the Nazca Lines, measures 3,860 feet (1,176 meters) from the base to the summit

- Cusco is home to some 350, 000 people today, it was founded as the capital of the ancient Inca Empire

- One of the most legendary archeological sites of all time, Machu Picchu is only about 50 miles from Cusco, but was not re-discovered until 1911, approximately 500 years after it was built and 400 years after it was abandoned, which is why it is also known as 'The Lost City of the Incas.'

Clothes & Shoe Sizes

Children's Shoe Sizes

UK	EUROPE	US	Japan
4	20	4½ or 5	12 ½
4 ½	21	5 or 5½	13
5	21 or 22	5½ or 6	13 ½
5 ½	22	6	13½ or 14
6	23	6½ or 7	14 or 14½
6 ½	23 or 24	7 ½	14½ or 15
7	24	7½ or 8	15
7 ½	25	8 or 9	15 ½
8	25 or 26	8½ or 9	16
8 ½	26	9½	16 ½
9	27	9½ or 10	16 ½ or 17
10	28	10½ or 11	17 ½
10½ or 11	29	11½ or 12	18
11 ½	30	12½	18 or 18 ½
12	31	13	19 or 19 ½
12 ½	31	13 or 13½	19 ½ or 20
13	32	1	20
13 ½	32 ½	1 ½	20 ½
1	33	1½ or 2	21
2	34	2½ or 3	22

Children's Clothing Sizes

UK	EUROPE	US	Australia
12m	80cm	12-18m	12m
18m	80-86cm	18-24m	18m
24m	86-92cm	23-24m	2
2-3	92-98cm	2T	3
3-4	98-104cm	4T	4
3-5	104-110cm	5	5
5-6	110-116cm	6	6
6-7	116-122cm	6X-7	7
7-8	122-128cm	7 to 8	8
8-9	128-134cm	9 to 10	9
9-10	134-140cm	10	10
10-11	140-146cm	11	11
11-12	146-152cm	14	12

Women's Shoe Sizes

UK	EUROPE	US	Japan
3	35 ½	5	22 ½
3 ½	36	5 ½	23
4	37	6	23
4 ½	37 ½	6 ½	23 ½
5	38	7	24
5 ½	39	7 ½	24
6	39 ½	8	24 ½
6 ½	40	8 ½	25
7	41	9 ½	25 ½
7 ½	41 ½	10	26
8	42	10 ½	26 ½

Women's Clothes Sizes

UK	US	Japan	France / Spain	Germany	Peru	Australia
6/8	6	7-9	36	34	40	8
10	8	9-11	38	36	42	10
12	10	11-13	40	38	44	12
14	12	13-15	42	39	46	14
16	14	15-17	44	40	48	16
18	16	17-19	46	42	50	18
20	18	19-21	48	44	52	20

Men's Shoe Sizes

UK	EUROPE	US	Japan
6	38 ½	6 ½	24 ½
6 ½	39	7	25
7	40	7 ½	25 ½
7 ½	41	8	26
8	42	8 ½	27 ½
8 ½	43	9	27 ½
9	43 ½	9 ½	28
9 ½	44	10	28 ½
10	44	10 ½	28 ½
10 ½	44 ½	11	29
11	45	12	29 ½

Men's Suit / Coat / Sweater Sizes

UK / US / Aus	EU / Japan	General
32	42	Small
34	44	Small
36	46	Small
38	48	Medium
40	50	Large
42	52	Large
44	54	Extra Large
46	56	Extra Large

Men's Pants / Trouser Sizes (Waist)

UK / US	Europe
32	81 cm
34	86 cm
36	91 cm
38	97 cm
40	102 cm
42	107 cm

We have included another copy of this at the back of the book, so you can find it quickly again when you are in Peru

Peru Trip Diary

Write a daily diary during your trip

Day 1

Date: **Weather:**

Day 2

Date: **Weather:**

Day 3

Date: June 3rd, 2018   **Weather:** _____

I've been on the plane to Lima since 5:00 pm. It is now 12:30 Am. The airport was nice, Dr. Scott was super helpful. I was nervous the whole day. I did not want to get lost or lose my luggage. I'm still nervous. I've never been this far from home and my anxiety is bad. I still have to tell everyone about my tourrettes which will be hard. I'm really tired. I also worry about having enough food and water. I brought Pinky with which calms me down. I have been reading the Peru travel guide books I brought.

Day 4

Date: _____ **Weather:** _____

Day 5

Tip! Send your postcards

Date: **Weather:**

Day 6

Date: _____   **Weather:** _____

Day 7

Date: _____   **Weather:** _____

Day 8

Date: **Weather:**

Day 9

Date: _____ **Weather:** _____

Day 10

Date: _____   **Weather:** _____

Day 11

Date: **Weather:**

Day 12

Date: **Weather:**

Day 13

Date: _____ Weather: _____

Day 14

Date: Weather:

Day 15

Date:	Weather:

Day 16

Date: Weather:

Day 17

Date: **Weather:**

Day 18

Date: **Weather:**

Day 19

Date: Weather:

Day 20

Date: **Weather:**

Day 21

Date: _____   Weather: _____

Memories of your Trip

Things I will remember from the trip

Favorite Places visited on the Trip

People I Met

Name:
Address:
Tel:
email:

Name:
Address:
Tel:
email:

Name:
Address:
Tel:
email:

Name:
Address:
Tel:
email:

Name:
Address:
Tel:
email:

Name:
Address:
Tel:
email:

Name:
Address:
Tel:
email:

Name:	
Address:	
Tel:	
email:	

Name:	
Address:	
Tel:	
email:	

Name:	
Address:	
Tel:	
email:	

Name:	
Address:	
Tel:	
email:	

We hope you enjoyed your trip to Peru

Please leave us a review if you found this Journal useful

Check out our useful resources on the next few pages

Clothes & Shoe Sizes

Children's Shoe Sizes

UK	EUROPE	US	Japan
4	20	4½ or 5	12 ½
4 ½	21	5 or 5½	13
5	21 or 22	5½ or 6	13 ½
5 ½	22	6	13½ or 14
6	23	6½ or 7	14 or 14½
6 ½	23 or 24	7 ½	14½ or 15
7	24	7½ or 8	15
7 ½	25	8 or 9	15 ½
8	25 or 26	8½ or 9	16
8 ½	26	9½	16 ½
9	27	9½ or 10	16 ½ or 17
10	28	10½ or 11	17 ½
10½ or 11	29	11½ or 12	18
11 ½	30	12½	18 or 18 ½
12	31	13	19 or 19 ½
12 ½	31	13 or 13½	19 ½ or 20
13	32	1	20
13 ½	32 ½	1 ½	20 ½
1	33	1½ or 2	21
2	34	2½ or 3	22

Children's Clothing Sizes

UK	EUROPE	US	Australia
12m	80cm	12-18m	12m
18m	80-86cm	18-24m	18m
24m	86-92cm	23-24m	2
2-3	92-98cm	2T	3
3-4	98-104cm	4T	4
3-5	104-110cm	5	5
5-6	110-116cm	6	6
6-7	116-122cm	6X-7	7
7-8	122-128cm	7 to 8	8
8-9	128-134cm	9 to 10	9
9-10	134-140cm	10	10
10-11	140-146cm	11	11
11-12	146-152cm	14	12

Women's Shoe Sizes

UK	EUROPE	US	Japan
3	35 ½	5	22 ½
3 ½	36	5 ½	23
4	37	6	23
4 ½	37 ½	6 ½	23 ½
5	38	7	24
5 ½	39	7 ½	24
6	39 ½	8	24 ½
6 ½	40	8 ½	25
7	41	9 ½	25 ½
7 ½	41 ½	10	26
8	42	10 ½	26 ½

Women's Clothes Sizes

UK	US	Japan	France / Spain	Germany	Peru	Australia
6/8	6	7-9	36	34	40	8
10	8	9-11	38	36	42	10
12	10	11-13	40	38	44	12
14	12	13-15	42	39	46	14
16	14	15-17	44	40	48	16
18	16	17-19	46	42	50	18
20	18	19-21	48	44	52	20

Men's Shoe Sizes

UK	EUROPE	US	Japan
6	38 ½	6 ½	24 ½
6 ½	39	7	25
7	40	7 ½	25 ½
7 ½	41	8	26
8	42	8 ½	27 ½
8 ½	43	9	27 ½
9	43 ½	9 ½	28
9 ½	44	10	28 ½
10	44	10 ½	28 ½
10 ½	44 ½	11	29
11	45	12	29 ½

Men's Suit / Coat / Sweater Sizes

UK / US / Aus	EU / Japan	General
32	42	Small
34	44	Small
36	46	Small
38	48	Medium
40	50	Large
42	52	Large
44	54	Extra Large
46	56	Extra Large

Men's Pants / Trouser Sizes (Waist)

UK / US	Europe
32	81 cm
34	86 cm
36	91 cm
38	97 cm
40	102 cm
42	107 cm

Common Translations

English	French	Spanish	Italian
Hello	Bonjour	Hola	Ciao
Goodbye	Au revoir	Adiós	Arrivederci
Yes	Oui	Sí	Si
No	Non	No	No
Please	S'il-vous-plaît	Por favor	Per favore
Thank you	Merci	Gracias	Grazie
Excuse me	Excusez-moi	Perdón	Mi scusi
How much	Combien	Cuánto	Quanto
My name is	Mon nom est	Mi nombre es	Io mi chiamo
Where is	Où est	Dónde está	Dov'è
The bank	La banque	El banco	La banca
The toilet	Les toilettes	El baño	Il bagno

German	Japanese	Mandarin	Hindi
Hallo	Kon'nichiwa	Ni hao	Namaste
Auf Wiedersehen	Sayonara	Zaijian	Alavida
Ja	Hai	Shi de	Ham
Nein	Ie	Meiyou	Nahim
Bitte	Onegaishimasu	Qing	Krpaya
Vielen Dank	Arigato	Xiexie	Dhan'yavada
Entschuldigung	Sumimasen	Duoshao	Mujhe mapha karem
Wie viel	Ikura	Wo de mingzi shi	Kitana
Mein Name ist	Watashinonamaeha	Nali	Mera nama hai
Wo ist	Doko ni aru	Yinhang	Kaham hai
Die Bank	Ginko	Yinhang	Bainka
Die Toilette	Toire	Cesuo	Saucalaya

Notes:

Made in the USA
Columbia, SC
01 February 2018